OF PATIENCE

Tertullian

Table of Contents

OF PATIENCE.

Tertullian

OF PATIENCE.

(TRANSLATED BY THE REV. S. THELWALL.)

OF PATIENCE.

CHAP. I.—OF PATIENCE GENERALLY; AND TERTULLIAN'S OWN UNWORTHINESS TO TREAT OF IT.

I FULLY confess unto the Lord God that it has been rash enough, if not even impudent, in me to have dared compose a treatise on Patience, for practising which I am all unfit, being a man of no goodness;[2] whereas it were becoming that such as have addressed themselves to the demonstration and commendation of some particular thing, should themselves first be conspicuous in the practice of that thing, and should regulate the constancy of their commonishing by the authority of their personal conduct, for fear their words blush at the deficiency of their deeds. And would that this "blushing" would bring a remedy, so that shame for not exhibiting that which we go to suggest to others should prove a tutorship into exhibiting it; except that the magnitude of some good things—just as of some ills too—is insupportable, so that only the grace of divine inspiration is effectual for attaining and practising them. For what is most good rests most with God; nor does any other than He who possesses it dispense it, as He deems meet to each. And so to discuss about that which it is not given one to enjoy, will be, as it were, a solace; after the manner of invalids, who since they are without health, know not how to be silent about its blessings. So I, most miserable, ever sick with the heats of impatience, must of necessity sigh after, and invoke, and persistently plead for, that health of patience which I possess not; while I recall to mind, and, in the contemplation of my own weakness, digest, the truth, that the good health of faith, and the soundness of the Lord's discipline, accrue not easily to any unless patience sit by his side.[3] So is patience set over the things of God, that one can obey no precept, fulfil no work well–pleasing to the Lord, if estranged from it. The good of it, even they who live outside it,[4] honour with the name of highest virtue. Philosophers indeed, who are accounted animals of some considerable wisdom, assign it so high a place, that, while they are mutually at discord with the various fancies of their sects and rivalries of their sentiments, yet, having a community of regard for patience alone, to this one of their pursuits they have joined in granting peace: for it they conspire; for it they league; it, in their affectation of[5] virtue, they unanimously pursue; concerning patience they exhibit all their ostentation of wisdom. Grand testimony this is to it, in that it incites even the vain schools of the world[6] unto praise and glory ! Or is it rather an injury, in that a thing divine is bandied among worldly sciences? But let them look to that, who shall presently be ashamed of their wisdom, destroyed and disgraced together with the world[7] (it lives in).

CHAP. II.—GOD HIMSELF AN EXAMPLE OF PATIENCE.

To us[8] no human affectation of canine[9] equanimity, modelled[10] by insensibility, furnishes the warrant for exercising patience; but the divine arrangement of a living and celestial discipline, holding up before us God Himself in the very first place as an example of patience; who scatters equally over just and unjust the bloom of this light; who suffers the good offices of the seasons, the services of the elements, the tributes of entire nature, to accrue at once to worthy and unworthy; bearing with the most ungrateful nations, adoring as they do the toys of the arts and the works of their own hands, persecuting His Name together with His family; bearing with luxury, avarice, iniquity, malignity, waxing insolent daily:[1] so that by His own patience He disparages Himself; for the cause why many believe not in the Lord is that they are so long without knowing[2] that He is wroth with the world.[3]

CHAP.III.—JESUS CHRIST IN HIS INCARNATION AND WORK A MORE IMITABLE EXAMPLE THEREOF.

And this species of the divine patience indeed being, as it were, at a distance, may perhaps be esteemed as among "things too high for us; "[4] but what is that which, in a certain way, has been grasped by hand[5] among men openly on the earth? God suffers Himself to be conceived in a mother's womb, and awaits the time for birth; and, when born, bears the delay of growing up; and, when grown up, is not eager to be recognised, but is furthermore contumelious to Himself, and is baptized by His own servant; and repels with words alone the assaults of the tempter; while from being" Lord" He becomes" Master," teaching man to escape death, having been trained to the exercise of the absolute forbearance of offended patience.[6] He did not strive; He did not cry aloud; nor did any hear His voice in the streets. He did not break the bruised reed; the smoking flax He did not quench: for the prophet—nay, the attestation of God Himself, placing His own Spirit, together with patience in its entirety, in His Son—had not falsely spoken. There was none desirous of cleaving to Him whom He did not receive. No one's table or roof did He despise: indeed, Himself ministered to the washing of the disciples' feet; not sinners, not publicans, did He repel; not with that city even which had refused to receive Him was He wroth,[7] when even the disciples had wished that the celestial fires should be forthwith hurled on so contumelious a town. He cared for the ungrateful; He yielded to His ensnarers. This were a small matter, if He had not had in His company even His own betrayer, and stedfastly abstained from pointing him out. Moreover, while He is being betrayed, while He is being led up "as a sheep for a victim," (for "so He no more opens His mouth than a lamb under the power of the shearer,")He to whom, had He willed it, legions of angels would at one word have presented themselves from the heavens, approved not the avenging sword of even one disciple The patience of the Lord was wounded in (the wound of) Malchus. And so, too, He cursed for the time to come the works of the sword; and, by the restoration of health, made satisfaction to him whom Himself had not hurt, through Patience, the mother of Mercy. I pass by in silence (the fact) that He is crucified, for this was the end for which He had come; yet had the death which must be undergone need of contumelies likewise?[8] Nay, but, when about to depart, He wished to be sated with the pleasure of patience. He is spitted on, scourged, derided, clad foully, more foully crowned. Wondrous is the faith of equanimity! He who had set before Him the concealing of Himself in man's shape, imitated nought of man's impatience ! Hence, even more than from any other trait, ought ye, Pharisees, to have recognised the Lord. Patience of this kind none of men would achieve. Such and so mighty evidences—the very magnitude of which proves to be among the nations indeed a cause for rejection of the faith, but among us its reason and rearing—proves manifestly enough (not by the sermons only, in enjoining, but likewise by the sufferings of the Lord in enduring) to them to whom it is given to believe, that as the effect and excellence of some inherent propriety, patience is God's nature.

CHAP. IV.—DUTY OF IMITATING OUR MASTER TAUGHT US BY SLAVES. EVEN BY BEASTS. OBEDIENT IMITATION IS FOUNDED ON PATIENCE.

Therefore, if we see all servants of probity and right feeling shaping their conduct suitably to the disposition of their lord; if, that is, the art of deserving favour is obedience,[9] while the rule of obedience is a compliant subjection: how much more does it behove us to be found with a character in accordance with our Lord,—servants as we are of the living God, whose judgment on His servants turns not on a fetter or a cap of freedom, but on an eternity either of penalty or of salvation; for the shunning of which severity or the courting of which liberality there needs a diligence in obedience[1] as great as are the comminations themselves which the severity utters, or the promises which the liberality freely makes.[2] And yet we exact obedience[3] not from men only, who have the bond of their slavery under their chin,[4] or in any other legal way are debtors to obedience? but even from cattle,[6] even from brutes;[7] understanding that they have been provided and delivered for our uses by the Lord. Shall, then, creatures which God makes subject to us be better than we in the discipline of obedience?[8] Finally, (the creatures) which obey, acknowledge their masters. Do we hesitate to listen diligently to Him to whom alone we are subjected—that is, the Lord? But how unjust is it, how ungrateful likewise, not to repay from yourself the same which, through the indulgence of your neighbour, you obtain from others, to him through whom you obtain it! Nor needs there more words on the exhibition of obedience[9] due from us to the Lord God; for the acknowledgment[10] of God understands what is incumbent on it. Lest, however, we seem to have inserted remarks on obedience[11] as something irrelevant, (let us remember) that obedience" itself is drawn from patience. Never does an impatient man render it, or a patient fail to find pleasure[12] in it. Who, then, could treat largely (enough) of the good of that patience which the Lord God, the Demonstrator and Acceptor of all good things, carried about in His own self?[13] To whom, again, would it be doubtful that every good thing ought, because it pertains[13] to God, to be earnestly pursued with the whole mind by such as pertain to God? By means of which (considerations) both commendation and exhortation[14] on the subject of patience are briefly, and as it were in the compendium of a prescriptive rule, established.[15]

OF PATIENCE.

CHAP, V.—AS GOD IS THE AUTHOR OF PATIENCE SO THE DEVIL IS OF IMPATIENCE.

Nevertheless, the proceeding[16] of a discussion on the necessaries of faith is not idle, because it is not unfruitful. In edification no loquacity is base, if it be base at any time.[19] And so, if the discourse be concerning some particular good, the subject requires us to review also the contrary of that good. For you will throw more light on what is to be pursued, if you first give a digest of what is to be avoided.

Let us therefore consider, concerning Impatience, whether just as patience in God, so its adversary quality have been born and detected in our adversary, that from this consideration may appear how primarily adverse it is to faith. For that which has been conceived by God's rival, of course is not friendly to God's things. The discord of things is the same as the discord of their authors. Further, since God is best, the devil on the contrary worst, of beings, by their own very diversity they testify that neither works for[18] the other; so that anything of good can no more seem to be effected for us by the Evil One, than anything of evil by the Good. Therefore I detect the nativity of impatience in the devil himself, at that very time when he impatiently bore that the Lord God subjected the universal works which He had made to His own image, that is, to man.[19] For if he had endured (that), he would not have grieved; nor would he have envied man if he had not grieved. Accordingly he deceived him, because he had envied him; but he had envied because he had grieved: he had grieved because, of course, he had not patiently borne. What that angel of perdition" first was—malicious or impatient—I scorn to inquire: since manifest it is that either impatience took its rise together with malice, or else malice from impatience; that subsequently they conspired between themselves; and that they grew up indivisible in one paternal bosom. But, however, having been instructed, by his own experiment, what an aid unto sinning was that which he had been the first to feel, and by means of which he had entered on his course of delinquency, he called the same to his assistance for the thrusting of man into crime. The woman,[1] immediately on being met by him—I may say so without rashness—was, through his very speech with her, breathed on by a spirit infected with impatience: so certain is it that she would never have sinned at all, if she had honoured the divine edict by maintaining her patience to the end. What (of the fact) that she endured not to have been met alone; but in the presence of Adam, not yet her husband, not yet bound to lend her his ears,[2] she is impatient of keeping silence, and makes him the transmitter of that which she had imbibed from the Evil One? Therefore another human being, too, perishes through the impatience of the one; presently, too, perishes of himself, through his own impatience committed in each respect, both in regard of God's premonition and in regard of the devil's cheatery; not enduring to observe the former nor to refute the latter. Hence, whence (the origin) of delinquency, arose the first origin of judgment; hence, whence man was induced to offend, God began to be wroth. Whence (came)the first indignation in God, thence (came) His first patience; who, content at that time with malediction only, refrained in the devil's case from the instant infliction[3] of punishment. Else what crime, before this guilt of impatience, is imputed to man? Innocent he was, and in intimate friendship with God, and the husbandman[4] of paradise. But when once he succumbed to impatience, he quite ceased to be of sweet savour[5] to God; he quite ceased to be able to endure things celestial. Thenceforward, a creature[6] given to earth, and ejected from the sight of God, he begins to be easily turned by impatience unto every use offensive to God. For straightway that impatience conceived of the devil's seed, produced, in the fecundity of malice, anger as her son; and when brought forth, trained him in her own arts. For that very thing which had immersed Adam and Eve in death, taught their son, too, to begin with murder. It would be idle for me to ascribe this to impatience, if Cain, that first homicide and first fratricide, had borne with equanimity and not impatiently the refusal by the Lord of his own oblations—if he is not wroth with his own brother—if, finally, he took away no one's life. Since, then, he could neither have killed unless he had been wroth, nor have been wroth unless he had been impatient, he demonstrates that what he did through wrath must be referred to that by which wrath was suggested during this cradle–time of impatience, then (in a certain sense) in her infancy. But how great presently were her augmentations ! And no wonder, If she has been the first delinquent, it is a consequence that, because she has been the first, therefore she is the only parent stem,[7] too, to every delinquency, pouring down from her own fount various veins of crimes.[8] Of murder we have spoken; but, being from the very beginning the outcome of anger,[9] whatever causes besides it shortly found for itself it lays collectively on the account of impatience, as to its own origin. For whether from private enmities, or for the sake of prey, any one perpetrates that wickedness,[10] the earlier step is his becoming impatient of" either the hatred or the avarice. Whatever compels a man, it is not possible that without impatience of itself it can be perfected in deed. Who ever committed adultery without impatience of lust? Moreover, if in females the sale of their modesty is forced by the price, of course it is by impatience of contemning gain[12] that this sale is regulated.[13] These (I mention) as the principal delinquencies in the sight of the

OF PATIENCE.

Lord,[14] for, to speak compendiously, every sin is ascribable to impatience. "Evil" is "impatience of good." None immodest is not impatient of modesty; dishonest of honesty; impious of piety;[15] unquiet of quietness. In order that each individual may become evil he will be unable to persevere[16] in being good. How, therefore, can such a hydra of delinquencies fail to offend the Lord, the Disapprover of evils? Is it not manifest that it was through impatience that Israel himself also always failed in his duty toward God, from that time when,[17] forgetful of the heavenly arm whereby he had been drawn out of his Egyptian affliction, he demands from Aaron "gods[18] as his guides;" when he pours down for an idol the contributions of his gold: for the so necessary delays of Moses, while he met with God, he had borne with impatience. After the edible rain of the manna, after the watery following[1] of the rock, they despair of the Lord in not enduring a three−days' thirst;[2] for this also is laid to their charge by the Lord as impatience. And—not to rove through individual cases—there was no instance in which it was not by failing in duty through impatience that they perished. How, moreover, did they lay hands on the prophets, except through impatience of hearing them? on the Lord moreover Himself, through impatience likewise of seeing Him? But had they entered the path of patience, they would have been set free.[3]

CHAP. VI.—PATIENCE BOTH ANTECEDENT AND SUBSEQUENT TO FAITH.

Accordingly it is patience which is both subsequent and antecedent to faith. In short, Abraham believed God, and was accredited by Him with righteousness;[4] but it was patience which proved his faith, when he was bidden to immolate his son, with a view to (I would not say the temptation, but) the typical attestation of his faith. But God knew whom He had accredited with righteousness.[3] So heavy a precept, the perfect execution whereof was not even pleasing to the Lord, he patiently both heard, and (if God had willed) would have fulfilled. Deservedly then was he "blessed." because he was "faithful;" deservedly "faithful," because "patient." So faith, illumined by patience, when it was becoming propagated among the nations through" Abraham's seed, which is Christ,"[6] and was superinducing grace over the law,[7] made patience her pre–eminent coadjutrix for amplifying and fulfilling the law, because that alone had been lacking unto the doctrine of righteousness. For men were of old wont to require "eye for eye, and tooth for tooth"[8] and to repay with usury "evil with evil; " for, as yet, patience was not on earth, because faith was not either. Of course, meantime, impatience used to enjoy the opportunities which the law gave. That was easy, while the Lord and Master of patience was absent. But after He has supervened, and has united[9] the grace of faith with patience, now it is no longer lawful to assail even with word, nor to say "fool"[20] even, without "danger of the judgment." Anger has been prohibited, our spirits retained, the petulance of the hand checked, the poison of the tongue[11] extracted. The law has found more than it has lost, while Christ says, "Love your personal enemies, and bless your cursers, and pray for your persecutors, that ye may be sons of your heavenly Father."[12] Do you see whom patience gains for us as a Father? In this principal precept the universal discipline of patience is succinctly comprised, since evil–doing is not conceded even when it is deserved.

CHAP.VII.—THE CAUSES OF IMPATIENCE, AND THEIR CORRESPONDENT PRECEPTS.

Now, however, while we run through the causes of impatience, all the other precepts also will answer in their own places. If our spirit is aroused by the loss of property, it is commonished by the Lord's Scriptures, in almost every place, to a contemning of the world;[13] nor is there any more powerful exhortation to contempt of money submitted[14] (to us), than (the fact) the Lord Himself is found amid no riches. He always justifies the poor, fore–condemns the rich. So He fore–ministered to patience "loss," and to opulence "contempt" (as portion);[15] demonstrating, by means of (His own) repudiation of riches, that hurts done to them also are not to be much regarded. Of that, therefore, which we have not the smallest need to seek after, because the Lord did not seek after it either, we ought to endure without heart–sickness the cutting down or taking away. "Covetousness," the Spirit of the Lord has through the apostle pronounced "a root of all evils."[16] Let us not interpret that covetousness as consisting merely in the concupiscence of what is another's: for even what seems ours is another's; for nothing is ours, since all things are God's, whose are we also ourselves. And so, if, when suffering from a loss, we feel impatiently, grieving for what is lost from what is not our own, we shall be detected as bordering on covetousness: we seek what is another's when we ill brook losing what is another's. He who is greatly stirred with impatience of a loss, does, by giving things earthly the precedence over things heavenly, sin directly[17] against God; for the Spirit, which he has received from the Lord, he greatly shocks for the sake of a worldly matter. Willingly, therefore, let us lose things earthly, let us keep things heavenly. Perish the whole world,[1] so I may make patience my gain! In truth, I know not whether he who has not made up his mind to endure with constancy the loss of somewhat of his, either by theft, or else by force, or else even by carelessness, would himself readily or heartily lay hand on his own property in the cause of almsgiving: for who that endures not at all to be cut by another, himself draws the sword on his own body? Patience in losses is an exercise in bestowing and communicating. Who fears not to lose, finds it not irksome to give. Else how will one, when he has two coats, give the one of them to the naked,[2] unless he be a man likewise to offer to one who takes away his coat his cloak as well?[3] How shall we fashion to us friends from mammon,[4] if we love it so much as not to put up with its loss? We shall perish together with the lost mammon. Why do we find here, where it is our business to lose?[3] To exhibit impatience at all losses is the Gentiles' business, who give money the precedence perhaps over their soul; for so they do, when, in their cupidities of lucre, they encounter the gainful perils of commerce on the sea; when, for money's sake, even in the forum, there is nothing which damnation (itself) would fear which they hesitate to essay; when they hire themselves for sport and the camp; when, after the manner of wild beasts, they play the bandit along the highway. But us, according to the diversity by which we are distinguished from them, it becomes to lay down not our soul for money, but money for our soul, whether spontaneously in bestowing or patiently in losing.

CHAP. VIII.—OF PATIENCE UNDER PERSONAL VIOLENCE AND MALEDICTION.

We who carry about our very soul, our very body, exposed in this world[6] to injury from all, and exhibit patience under that injury; shall we be hurt at the loss[7] of less important things?[8] Far from a servant of Christ be such a defilement as that the patience which has been prepared for greater temptations should forsake him in frivolous ones. If one attempt to provoke you by manual violence, the monition of the Lord is at hand: "To him," He saith, "who smiteth thee on the face, turn the other cheek likewise."[9] Let outrageousness[10] be wearied out by your patience. Whatever that blow may be, conjoined[11] with pain and contumely, it[12] shall receive a heavier one from the Lord. You wound that outrageous[13] one more by enduring: for he will be beaten by Him for whose sake you endure. If the tongue's bitterness break out in malediction or reproach, look back at the saying, "When they curse you, rejoice."[14] The Lord Himself was "cursed" in the eye of the law;[15] and yet is He the only Blessed One. Let us servants, therefore, follow our Lord closely; and be cursed patiently, that we may be able to be blessed. If I hear with too little equanimity some wanton or wicked word uttered against me, I must of necessity either myself retaliate the bitterness, or else I shall be racked with mute impatience. When, then, on being cursed, I smite (with my tongue,) how shall I be found to have followed the doctrine of the Lord, in which it has been delivered that "a man is defiled,[16] not by the defilements of vessels, but of the things which are sent forth out of his mouth." Again, it is said that "impeachment[17] awaits us for every vain and needless word."[18] It follows that, from whatever the Lord keeps us, the same He admonishes us to bear patiently from another. I will add (somewhat) touching the pleasure of patience. For every injury, whether inflicted by tongue or hand, when it has lighted upon patience, will be dismissed[19] with the same fate as, some weapon launched against and blunted on a rock of most stedfast hardness. For it will wholly fall then and there with bootless and fruitless labour; and sometimes will recoil and spend its rage on him who sent it out, with retorted impetus. No doubt the reason why any one hurts you is that you may be pained; because the hurter's enjoyment consists in the pain of the hurt. When, then, you have upset his enjoyment by not being pained, he must needs he pained by the loss of his enjoyment. Then you not only go unhurt away, which even alone is enough for you; but gratified, into the bargain, by your adversary's disappointment, and revenged by his pain. This is the utility and the pleasure of patience.

CHAP. IX.—OF PATIENCE UNDER BEREAVEMENT.

Not even that species of impatience under the loss of our dear ones is excused, where some assertion of a right to grief acts the patron to it. For the consideration of the apostle's declaration must be set before us, who says, "Be not overwhelmed with sadness at the falling asleep of any one, just as the nations are who are without hope."[1] And justly; or, believing the resurrection of Christ we believe also in our own, for whose sake He both died and rose again. Since, then, there is certainty as to the resurrection of the dead, grief for death is needless, and impatience of grief is needless. For why should you grieve, if you believe that (your loved one) is not perished? Why should you bear impatiently the temporary withdrawal of him who you believe will return? That which you think to be death is departure. He who goes before us is not to be lamented, though by all means to be longed for.[2] That longing also must be tempered with patience. For why should you bear without moderation the fact that one is gone away whom you will presently follow? Besides, impatience in matters of this kind bodes ill for our hope, and is a dealing insincerely with the faith. And we wound Christ when we accept not with equanimity the summoning out of this world of any by Him, as if they were to be pitied. "I desire," says the apostle, "to be now received, and to be with Christ."[3] How far better a desire does he exhibit! If, then, we grieve impatiently over such as have attained the desire of Christians, we show unwillingness ourselves to attain it.

CHAP. X.—OF REVENGE.

There is, too, another chief spur of impatience, the lust of revenge, dealing with the business either of glory or else of malice. But "glory," on the one hand, is everywhere "vain;"[4] and malice, on the other, is always[5] odious to the Lord; in this case indeed most of all, when, being provoked by a neighbour's malice, it constitutes itself superior[6] in following out revenge, and by paying wickedness doubles that which has once been done. Revenge, in the estimation of error,[7] seems a solace of pain; in the estimation of truth, on the contrary, it is convicted of malignity. For what difference is there between provoker and provoked, except that the former is detected as prior in evil–doing, but the latter as posterior? Yet each stands impeached of hurting a man in the eye of the Lord, who both prohibits and condemns every wickedness. In evil doing there is no account taken of order, nor does place separate what similarity conjoins. And the precept is absolute, that evil is not to be repaid with evil.[8] Like deed involves like merit. How shall we observe that principle, if in our loathing[9] we shall not loathe revenge? What honour, moreover, shall we be offering to the Lord God, if we arrogate to ourselves the arbitrament of vengeance? We are corrupt [10]—earthen vessels.[11] With our own servant–boys,[12] if they assume to themselves the right of vengeance on their fellow–servants, we are gravely offended; while such as make us the offering of their patience we not only approve as mindful of humility, of servitude, affectionately jealous of the right of their lord's honour; but we make them an ampler satisfaction than they would have pre–exacted[13] for themselves. Is there any risk of a different result in the case of a Lord so just in estimating, so potent in executing? Why, then, do we believe Him a Judge, if not an Avenger too? This He promises that He will be to us in return, saying, "Vengeance belongeth to me, and I will avenge; "[14] that is, Leave patience to me, and I will reward patience. For when He says, "Judge not, lest ye be judged,"[15] does He not require patience? For who will refrain from judging another, but he who shall be patient in not revenging himself? Who judges in order to pardon? And if he shall pardon, still he has taken care to indulge the impatience of a judger, and has taken away the honour of the one Judge, that is, God. How many mischances had impatience of this kind been wont to run into! How oft has it repented of its revenge! How oft has its vehemence been found worse than the causes which led to it!—inasmuch as nothing undertaken with impatience can be effected without impetuosity: nothing done with impetuosity fails either to stumble, or else to fall altogether, or else to vanish headlong.

OF PATIENCE.

Moreover, if you avenge yourself too slightly, you will be mad; if too amply, you will have to bear the burden.[1] What have I to do with vengeance, the measure of which, through impatience of pain, I am unable to regulate? Whereas, if I shall repose on patience, I shall not feel pain; if I shall not feel pain, I shall not desire to avenge myself.

CHAP. XI.—FURTHER REASONS FOR PRACTISING PATIENCE. ITS CONNECTION WITH THE BEATITUDES.

After these principal material causes of impatience, registered to the best of our ability, why should we wander out of our way among the rest,—what are found at home, what abroad? Wide and diffusive is the Evil One's operation, hurling manifold irritations of our spirit, and sometimes trifling ones, sometimes very great. But the trifling ones you may contemn from their very littleness; to the very great ones you may yield in regard of their overpoweringness. Where the injury is less, there is no necessity for impatience; but where the injury is greater, there more necessary is the remedy for the injury—patience. Let us strive, therefore, to endure the inflictions of the Evil One, that the counter–zeal of our equanimity may mock the zeal of the foe. If, however, we ourselves, either by imprudence or else voluntarily, draw upon ourselves anything, let us meet with equal patience what we have to blame ourselves for. Moreover, if we believe that some inflictions are sent on us by the Lord, to whom should we more exhibit patience than to the Lord? Nay, He teaches[2] us to give thanks and rejoice, over and above, at being thought worthy of divine chastisement. "Whom I love," saith He, "I chasten."[3] O blessed servant, on whose amendment the Lord is intent! with whom He deigns to be wroth! whom He does not deceive by dissembling His reproofs! On every side, therefore, we are bound to the duty of exercising patience, from whatever quarter, either by our own errors or else by the snares of the Evil One, we incur the Lord's reproofs. Of that duty great is the reward—namely, happiness. For whom but the patient has the Lord called happy, in saying, "Blessed are the poor in spirit, for theirs is the kingdom of the heavens?"[4] No one, assuredly, is "poor in spirit," except he be humble. Well, who is humble, except he be patient? For no one can abase himself without patience, in the first instance, to bear the act of abasement. "Blessed," saith He, "are the weepers and mourners."[5] Who, without patience, is tolerant of such unhappinesses? And so to such, "consolation" and "laughter" are promised. "Blessed are the gentle:"[6] under this term, surely, the impatient cannot possibly be classed. Again, when He marks "the peacemakers"[7] with the same title of felicity, and names them "sons of God," pray have the impatient any affinity with "peace?" Even a fool may perceive that. When, however, He says, "Rejoice and exult, as often as they shall curse and persecute you; for very great is your reward in heaven,"[8] of course it is not to the patience of exultation[9] that He makes that promise; because no one will "exult" in adversities unless he have first learnt to contemn them; no one will contemn them unless he have learnt to practise patience.

CHAP. XII.—CERTAIN OTHER DIVINE PRECEPTS. THE APOSTOLIC DESCRIPTION OF CHARITY. THEIR CONNECTION WITH PATIENCE.

As regards the rule of peace, which[10] is so pleasing to God, who in the world that is prone to impatience[11] will even once forgive his brother, I will not say "seven times," or[12] "seventy–seven times?"[13] Who that is contemplating a suit against his adversary will compose the matter by agreement,[14] unless he first begin by lopping off chagrin, hardheartedness, and bitterness, which are in fact the poisonous outgrowths of impatience? How will you "remit, and remission shall be granted" you? if the absence of patience makes you tenacious of a wrong? No one who is at variance with his brother in his mind, will finish offering his "duteous gift at the altar," unless he first, with intent to "re–conciliate his brother," return to patience.[16] If "the sun go down over our wrath," we are in jeopardy:[17] we are not allowed to remain one day without patience. But, however, since Patience takes the lead in[18] every species of salutary discipline, what wonder that she likewise ministers to Repentance, (accustomed as Repentance is to come to the rescue of such as have fallen,) when, on a disjunction of wedlock (for that cause, I mean, which makes it lawful, whether for husband or wife, to persist in the perpetual observance of widowhood),[1] she[2] waits for, she yearns for, she persuades by her entreaties, repentance in all who are one day to enter salvation? How great a blessing she confers on each! The one she prevents from becoming an adulterer; the other she amends. So, to, she is found in those holy examples touching patience in the Lord's parables. The shepherd's patience seeks and finds the straying ewe:[3] for Impatience would easily despise one ewe; but Patience undertakes the labour of the quest, and the patient burden–bearer carries home on his shoulders the forsaken sinner.[4] That prodigal son also the father's patience receives, and clothes, and feeds, and makes excuses for, in the presence of the angry brother's impatience.[5] He, therefore, who "had perished" is saved, because he entered on the way of repentance. Repentance perishes not, because it finds Patience (to welcome it). For by whose teachings but those of Patience is Charity[6]—the highest sacrament of the faith, the treasure–house of the Christian name, which the apostle commends with the whole strength of the Holy Spirit—trained? "Charity," he says, "is long suffering;" thus she applies patience: "is beneficent;" Patience does no evil: "is not emulous;" that certainly is a peculiar mark of patience: "savours not of violence:"[7] she has drawn her self–restraint from patience: "is not puffed up; is not violent;"[8] for that pertains not unto patience: "nor does she seek her own" if, she offers her own, provided she may benefit her neighbours: "nor is irritable;" if she were, what would she have left to Impatience? Accordingly he says, "Charity endures all things; tolerates all things;" of course because she is patient. Justly, then, "will she never fail;"[9] for all other things will be cancelled, will have their consummation. "Tongues, sciences, prophecies, become exhausted; faith, hope, charity, are permanent:" Faith, which Christ's patience introduced; hope, which man's patience waits for; charity, which Patience accompanies, with God as Master.

CHAP. XIII.—OF BODILY PATIENCE.

Thus far, finally, of patience simple and uniform, and as it exists merely in the mind: though in many forms likewise I labour after it in body, for the purpose of "winning the Lord;"[10] inasmuch as it is a quality which has been exhibited by the Lord Himself in bodily virtue as well; if it is true that the ruling mind easily communicates the gifts" of the Spirit with its bodily habitation. What, therefore, is the business of Patience in the body? In the first place, it is the affliction[12] of the flesh—a victim[13] able to appease the Lord by means of the sacrifice of humiliation—in making a libation to the Lord of sordid[14] raiment, together with scantiness of food, content with simple diet and the pure drink of water[15] in con joining fasts to all this; in inuring herself to sackcloth and ashes. This bodily patience adds a grace to our prayers for good, a strength to our prayers against evil; this opens the ears of Christ our God,[16] dissipates severity, elicits clemency. Thus that Babylonish king,[17] after being exiled from human form in his seven years' squalor and neglect., because he had offended the Lord; by the bodily immolation of patience not only recovered his kingdom, but—what is more to be desired by a man—made satisfaction to God. Further, if we set down in order the higher and happier grades of bodily patience, (we find that)it is she who is entrusted by holiness with the care of continence of the flesh: she keeps the widow,[18] and sets on the virgin the seal[19] and raises the self–made eunuch to the realms of heaven.[20] That which springs from a virtue of the mind is perfected in the flesh; and, finally, by the patience of the flesh, does battle under persecution. If flight press hard, the flesh wars with[21] the inconvenience of flight; if imprisonment over– take[2] us, the flesh (still was) in bonds, the flesh in the gyve, the flesh in solitude, and in that want of light, and in that patience of the world's misusage.[3] When, however, it is led forth unto the final proof of happiness,[4] unto the occasion of the second baptism,[5] unto the act of ascending the divine seat, no patience is more needed there than badly patience. If the "spirit is willing, but the flesh," without patience, "weak,"[6] where, save in patience, is the safety of the spirit, and of the flesh itself? But when the Lord says this about the flesh, pronouncing it "weak," He shows what need there is of strengthening, it—that is by patience—to meet[7] every preparation for subverting or punishing faith; that it may bear with all constancy stripes, fire, cross, beasts, sword; all which prophets and apostles, by enduring, conquered!

CHAP. XIV.—THE POWER OF THIS TWOFOLD PATIENCE, THE SPIRITUAL AND THE BODILY. EXEMPLIFIED IN THE SAINTS OF OLD.

With this strength of patience, Esaias is cut asunder, and ceases not to speak concerning the Lord; Stephen is stoned, and prays for pardon to his foes.[8] Oh, happy also he who met all the violence of the devil by the exertion of every species of patience! [9]—whom neither the driving away of his cattle nor those riches of his in sheep, nor the sweeping away of his children in one swoop of ruin, nor, finally, the agony of his own body in (one universal) wound, estranged from the patience and the faith which he had plighted to the Lord; whom the devil smote with all his might in vain. For by all his pains he was not drawn away from his reverence for God; but he has been set up as an example and testimony to us, for the thorough accomplishment of patience as well in spirit as in flesh, as well in mind as in body; in order that we succumb neither to damages of our worldly goods, nor to losses of those who are dearest, nor even to bodily afflictions. What a bier[10] for the devil did God erect in the person of that hero! What a banner did He rear over the enemy of His glory, when, at every bitter message, that man uttered nothing out of his mouth but thanks to God, while he denounced his wife, now quite wearied with ills, and urging him to resort to crooked remedies! How did God smile,[11] how was the evil one cut asunder,[12] while Job with mighty equanimity kept scraping off[13] the unclean overflow of his own ulcer, while he sportively replaced the vermin that brake out thence, in the same caves and feeding–places of his pitted flesh! And so, when all the darts of temptations had blunted themselves against the corslet and shield of his patience, that instrument[14] of God's victory not only presently recovered from God the soundness of his body, but possessed in redoubled measure what he had lost. And if he had wished to have his children also restored, he might again have been called father; but he preferred to have them restored him "in that day."[15] · Such joy as that —secure so entirely concerning the Lord—he deferred; meantime he endured a voluntary bereavement, that he might not live without some (exercise of) patience.

CHAP. XV.—GENERAL SUMMARY OF THE VIRTUES AND EFFECTS OF PATIENCE.

So amply sufficient a Depositary of patience is God. If it be a wrong which you deposit in His care, He is an Avenger; if a loss, He is a Restorer; if pain, He is a Healer; if death, He is a Reviver. What honour is granted to Patience, to have God as her Debtor! And not without reason: for she keeps all His decrees; she has to do with all His mandates. She fortifies faith; is the pilot of peace; assists charity; establishes humility; waits long for repentance; sets tier seal on confession; rules the flesh; preserves the spirit; bridles the tongue; restrains the hand; tramples temptations under foot; drives away scandals; gives their crowning grace to martyrdoms; consoles the poor; teaches the rich moderation; overstrains not the weak; exhausts not the strong; is the delight of the believer; invites the Gentile; commends the servant to his lord, and his lord to God; adorns the woman; makes the man approved; is loved in childhood, praised in youth, looked up to in age; is beauteous in either sex, in every time of life. Come, now, see whether[16] we have a general idea of her mien and habit. Her countenance is tranquil and peaceful; her brow serene[17] contracted by no wrinkle of sadness or of anger; her eyebrows evenly relaxed in gladsome wise, with eyes downcast in humility, not in unhappiness; her mouth sealed with the honourable mark of silence; her hue such as theirs who are without care and without guilt; the motion of her head frequent against the devil, and her laugh threatening;[1] her clothing, moreover, about her bosom white and well fitted to her person, as being neither inflated nor disturbed. For Patience sits on the throne of that calmest and gentlest Spirit, who is not found in the roll of the whirlwind, nor in the leaden hue of the cloud but is of soft serenity, open and simple, whom Elias saw at his third essay.[2] For where God is, there too is His foster–child, namely Patience. When God's Spirit descends, then Patience accompanies Him indivisibly. If we do not give admission to her together with the Spirit, will (He) always tarry with us? Nay, I know not whether He would remain any longer. Without His companion and handmaid, He must of necessity be straitened in every place and at every time. Whatever blow His enemy may inflict He will be unable to endure alone, being without the instrumental means of enduring.

CHAP. XVI.—THE PATIENCE OF THE HEATHEN VERY DIFFERENT FROM CHRISTIAN PATIENCE. THEIRS DOOMED TO PERDITION. OURS DESTINED TO SALVATION.

This is the rule, this the discipline, these the works of patience which is heavenly and true; that is, of Christian patience, not false and disgraceful, like as is that patience of the nations of the earth. For in order that in this also the devil might rival the Lord, he has as it were quite on a par (except that the very diversity of evil and good is exactly on a par with their magnitude[3]) taught his disciples also a patience of his own; that, I mean, which, making husbands venal for dowry, and teaching them to trade in panderings, makes them subject to the power of their wives; which, with feigned affection, undergoes. every toil of forced complaisance,[4] with a view to ensnaring the childless;[5] which makes the slaves of the belly[6] submit to contumelious patronage, in the subjection of their liberty to their gullet. Such pursuits of patience the Gentiles are acquainted with; and they eagerly seize a name of so great goodness to apply it to foul practises: patient they live of rivals, and of the rich, and of such as give them invitations; impatient of God alone. But let their own and their leader's patience look to itself—a patience which the subterraneous fire awaits! Let us, on the other hand, love the patience of God, the patience of Christ; let us repay to Him the patience which He has paid down for us! Let us offer to Him the patience of the spirit, the patience of the flesh, believing as we do in the resurrection of flesh and spirit.

ELUCIDATIONS.

I.

(Unless patience sit by his side, cap. i. p. 707.)

 Let me quote words which, many years ago, struck me forcibly, and which I trust, have been blest to my soul; for which reason, I must be allowed, here, to thank their author, the learned and fearless Dean Burgon, of Chichester. In his invaluable Commentary on the Gospel, which while it abounds in the fruits of a varied erudition, aims only to be practically useful, this pious scholar remarks: "To Faith must be added Patience, the 'patient waiting for God,' if we would escape the snare which Satan spread, no less for the Holy One (i.e. in the Temp. upon the Pinnacle)than for the Israelites at Massah. And this is perhaps the reason of the remarkable prominence given to the grace of Patience, both by our Lord and His Apostles; a circumstance, as it may be thought, which has not altogether attracted the attention which it deserves." He then cites examples;[1] but a reference to any good concordance will strikingly exemplify the admirable comment of this "godly and well–learned man." See his comments on St. Matt. iv. 7. and St. Luke xxi, 19.

II.

(Under their chin, cap. iv. p. 709.)

 The reference in the note to Paris, as represented by Virgil and in ancient sculpture, seems somewhat to the point

"Et nunc ille Paris, cure semiviro comitatu.
 Maeonia mentum mitra crinemq, madentem.

        Subnixus, etc."

OF PATIENCE.

He had just spoken of the pileus as a "Cap of freedom," but there was another form of pileus which was just the reverse and was probably tied by fimbria, under the chin, denoting a low order of slaves, effeminate men, perhaps spadones. Now, the Phrygian bonnet to which Virgil refers, is introduced by him to complete the reproach of his contemptuous expression (semiviro comitatu) just before. So, our author—"not only from men, i.e. men so degraded as to wear this badge of extreme servitude, but even from cattle, etc. Shall these mean creatures outdo us in obedience and patience?"

III.

(The world's misusage, cap. xiii. p. 716.)

The Reverend Clergy who may read this note will forgive a brother, who begins to be in respect of years, like "Paul the aged," for remarking, that the reading of the Ante–Nicene Fathers often leads him to sigh—"Such were they from whom we have received all that makes life tolerable, but how intolerable it was for them: are we, indeed, such as they would have considered Christians?" GOD be praised for His mercy and forbearance in our days; but, still it is true that "we have need of patience." Is not much of all that we regard as "the world's misusage," the gracious hand of the Master upon us, giving us something for the exercise of that Patience, by which He forms us into His own image? (Heb. xii. 3.) Impatience of obscurity, of poverty, of ingratitude, of misrepresentation, of "the slings and arrows" of slander and abuse, is a revolt against that indispensable discipline of the Gospel which requires us to "endure afflictions" in some form or other. Who can complain when one thinks what it would have cost us to be Christians in Tertullian's time? The ambition of the Clergy is always rebellion against God, and "patient waiting" is its only remedy. One will find profitable reading on this subject in Massillon[2] de l'Ambition des Clercs: "Reposez–vous sur le Seigneur du soin de votre destinee: il saura bien accomplir, tout seul, les desseins qu'il a sur vous. Si votre elccomplir, tout seul, les desseins qu'il a sur vous. Si votre ubevation est son bon plaisir, elle sera, aussi son ouvrage. Rendez–vous en digne seulement par la retraite, par la frayeur, par la fuite, par Its sentiments vifs de votre indignite ... c'est ainsi que les Chrysostome, les Gregoire, les Basil, les Augustin, furent donnes indes a l'Eglise."

27

Printed in the United States
47747LVS00004B/4

9 781419 137785